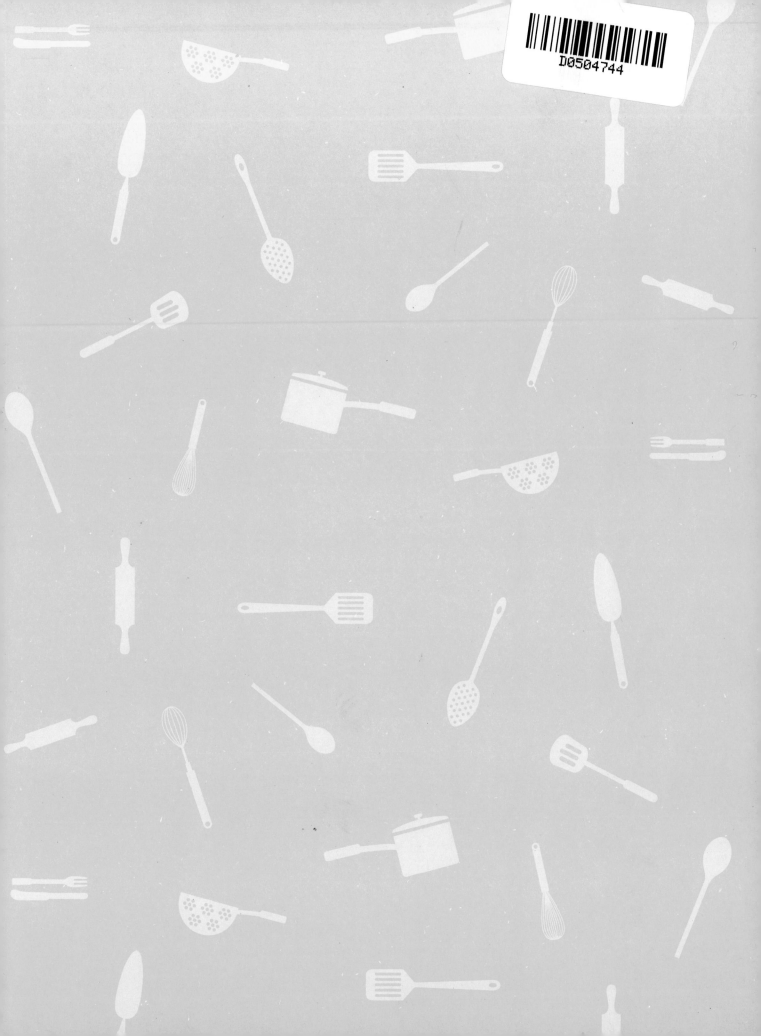

PARTY FOOD

BY NANCY LAMBERT

PUBLISHING PLC

Published by Top That! Publishing plc
Tide Mill Way, Woodbridge, Suffolk, IP12 IAP, UK
www.topthatpublishing.com
Copyright © 2012 Top That! Publishing plc

CONTENTS

INTRODUCTION

It's paaaaarrrrrty time! The venue, invitations, games and activities are sorted, so now it's time to plan the food! First, get organised – work out what you are going to cook beforehand and leave plenty of time so you don't feel rushed. If you can, cook some of the food the day before and keep it in the fridge!

If you are having a themed party, try to make the food as fun and relevant as you can. Why not try a princess, pirate, or witches and wizards party? Themed table decorations can also complement your food – and don't forget the party hats, banners and streamers!

This book will provide you with a selection of delicious party recipes for adults and junior chefs to make together. And remember, once you have perfected the recipes, don't be afraid to experiment with the ingredients, fillings and toppings to create and decorate your very own party treats!

COOKING TIPS!

- Make sure you use the freshest ingredients available.

- Prepare all the food that you can in advance.

- If you have any food left over, wrap it in brightly coloured napkins or paper and put it into party bags for your guests to take away.

- Provide lots of drinks for your guests, such as smoothies, squash and little bottles of water – preparing for and having a party can be thirsty work.

EQUIPMENT

- To complete the recipes in this book, you will need to use a selection of everyday cooking equipment and utensils, such as mixing bowls, saucepans, a sieve, knives, spoons and forks and a chopping board.

- Of course, you'll need to weigh and measure the ingredients, so you'll need a measuring jug and some kitchen scales too.

- To make some of the recipes in this book, you'll need to use special kitchen equipment. These items (and others that you may not have to hand) are listed at the start of each recipe.

SAFETY & HYGIENE

- Before starting any cooking always wash your hands.

- Cover any cuts with a plaster.

- Wear an apron to protect your clothes.

- Always make sure that all the equipment you use is clean.

- If you need to use a sharp knife to cut up something hard, ask an adult to help you. Always use a chopping board.

- Remember that trays in the oven and pans on the cooker can get very hot. Always ask an adult to turn on the oven and to get things in and out of the oven for you.

- Always ask an adult for help if you are using anything electrical – like an electric whisk.

- Be careful when heating anything in a pan on top of the cooker. Keep the handle turned to one side to avoid accidentally knocking the pan.

- Keep your pets out of the kitchen while cooking.

GETTING STARTED

MEASURING

Use scales to weigh exactly how much of each ingredient you need or use a measuring jug to measure liquids.

MIXING

Use a spoon, balloon whisk or electric hand whisk to mix the ingredients together.

CREATING RECIPES

Once you've made a recipe in this book a few times, think about whether you could make your own version. Don't be afraid to experiment with the recipes to find something you like. Try to think up names for the things you create!

PLEASE NOTE

The temperatures and measurements given in this book are approximate. Use the same measurement conversions throughout your recipe (grams or ounces) to maintain the correct ratios. All of the recipes in this book have been created for adults to make with junior chefs and must not be attempted by an unsupervised child.

Read through each recipe to make sure you've got all the ingredients that you need before you start.

MINI SAUSAGE ROLLS

TOP TIP!
Pile the sausage rolls on brightly coloured plates!

MAKES 10

Extra equipment:
- rolling pin
- pastry brush
- baking tray

Ingredients:
- 1 tablespoon butter
- 1 red onion, peeled and finely sliced
- 6 pork sausages
- a handful of breadcrumbs
- 2 tablespoons plain flour
- 250 g (9 oz) ready-made puff pastry
- 1 egg
- a little milk

1 Preheat the oven to 180°C / 350°F / gas mark 4.

2 Melt the butter in a saucepan and add the onions. Cook gently for about 20 minutes until soft. Then, spread out on a plate to cool.

3 Ask an adult to slit the skins of the sausages and pop the meat out. Put the meat in a mixing bowl with the onion and the breadcrumbs, and then scrunch well, with clean hands, to mix together.

4 On a floured work surface, roll the pastry out into a rectangle so it is about 1 cm (1/2 in.) thick. Then, cut it lengthways into two long, even rectangles.

5 Roll the mixture, made in step 3, into sausage shapes with your hands, and lay along the centre of each rectangle.

6 Mix the egg and milk and brush over the pastry. Then, fold one side of the pastry over the filling. Press down with your fingers or the edge of a spoon to seal.

7 Cut the long rolls into the size you want and space them out on a baking tray. Brush with the rest of the egg mix and bake for 25 minutes or until puffed and golden.

CHEESY PASTRIES

Extra equipment:
• baking tray
• baking parchment
• sieve
• rolling pin

Ingredients:
• 100 g (4 oz) butter, plus extra for greasing
• 150 g (5 oz) mature cheddar cheese, grated
• 100 g (4 oz) plain flour, plus extra for dusting the work surface
• 1 egg yolk

1 Preheat the oven to 180°C / 350°F / gas mark 4.

2 Lightly grease a baking tray with butter and cover it with a piece of baking parchment.

3 Put the cheese into a mixing bowl and sift in the flour. Next, cut the butter into little cubes and rub them into the mixture with your fingertips.

4 When you have a crumbly mixture, stir in the egg yolk.

5 Knead the mixture until it forms a dough. Then dust the work surface with plenty of flour. Roll out the dough into a square, until it is about 1 cm (1/2 in.) thick.

6 Ask an adult to cut the square into strips, then twist the strips or make them into circles or heart shapes. Gently lift them onto the baking tray.

7 Ask an adult to place the tray in a preheated oven and bake for about 8 minutes, until they are golden brown. Then, carefully transfer the pastries to a wire rack to cool.

TOP TIP!
Add tomato purée, prior to twisting, for a variation.

11

VEGGIE STICKS & DIPS

Extra equipment:
• blender

Ingredients:

For the dips:

Yogurt and Herb:
• 200 g (7 oz) natural yogurt
• 1 teaspoon each dill and mint, chopped

Marie Rose:
• 2 tablespoons mayonnaise
• 2 tablespoons crème fraîche
• 1 tablespoon tomato ketchup
• 1 teaspoon Worcester sauce
• 1 teaspoon lemon juice

For the sticks:
• a selection of fresh vegetables: carrots, celery, cucumber, peppers

For the dips:

1 Yogurt and Herb:
Mix the yogurt with the chopped herbs and serve!

2 Marie Rose:
Mix all of the ingredients together and serve!

For the veggie sticks:

1 First, wash and prepare the vegetables.

2 Ask an adult to help you peel and chop up the vegetables into sticks.

3 Now, scoop the dips into small bowls and serve with your veggie sticks!

TOP TIP!
Add freshly chopped chives to the marie rose dip for a taste sensation!

BITE-SIZED BURGERS

Ingredients:
- 1 kg (2 lb, 2 oz) minced beef
- 1 onion, finely chopped
- 4 tablespoons fine breadcrumbs
- 2 eggs, lightly beaten
- pinch of salt and pepper to season
- 1 teaspoon mustard
- 2 cloves garlic, peeled and crushed

To serve:
- mini burger buns (or bread cut to size)
- salad
- cheese, sliced

1 Preheat the grill / pan / barbecue to a medium heat.

2 Place the minced beef in a large bowl and add the remaining ingredients. Mix it all together, either with your hands or a spoon, until just combined.

3 Wet your hands, and then mould the mixture into burger shapes about 2 cm (1 in.) thick.

4 The burgers can now be cooked either on a griddle pan, non-stick frying pan with a dash of oil, under the grill or on a barbecue. Make sure you preheat the frying pan, griddle pan, grill or barbecue to a medium heat before placing the burgers on top.

5 Cook the burgers for about 4 minutes on each side, turning them once.

6 Serve with mini burger buns, salad and cheese (optional).

TOP TIP!
Why not add some home-made tomato salsa to your burger? Just chop up some fresh tomatoes, red onion, coriander and garlic!

GARLIC BREAD

Extra equipment:
- foil
- baking tray

Ingredients:
- 3 large garlic cloves, peeled and finely chopped
- 100 g (4 oz) softened butter
- 2 tablespoons flat-leaf parsley
- 1 small baguette

1 Preheat the oven to 180°C / 350°F / gas mark 4.

2 Mix the garlic and butter in a large bowl and then stir in the parsley.

3 Ask an adult to slice the baguette every 2.5 cm (1 in.) along its length (don't cut all the way through) and smear a large amount of the garlic butter into each slice.

4 Then, wrap the baguette in foil.

5 Ask an adult to place the wrapped bread on a baking tray and put into the oven to bake for 10 minutes.

6 Carefully unwrap the bread from the foil and open up.

7 Cut into portions and serve while it's still hot!

TOP TIP! Sprinkle some grated cheddar cheese on the bread 5 minutes before it's ready!

MINI PIZZAS

Extra equipment:
- rolling pin
- large cookie cutters

Ingredients:
- 290 g (10 oz) pizza base mix
- 100 ml (3½ fl.oz) warm water
- tomato purée
- mozzarella cheese
- basil or oregano (optional)
- any topping you like

1 Preheat the oven to 200°C / 400°F / gas mark 6.

2 Empty the pizza base mix into a bowl, add the water, and mix according to the packet instructions.

3 Using a rolling pin, roll the pizza mix dough so it is about 2 cm (1 in.) thick. Use large cookie cutters to cut out shapes.

4 Next, spread a thin layer of the tomato purée onto the base, then add the mozzarella cheese and the herbs.

5 Add the topping of your choice. Why not add a few different toppings, such as brie and cranberry or perhaps a sweet topping like pineapple!

6 Ask an adult to place the mini pizzas into a preheated oven for 10–15 minutes or until they are piping hot and the bases are golden brown.

TOP TIP!
Why not arrange the pizza toppings to make funny faces?

TOP TIP!
Separate the sandwiches if you know that there are vegetarians coming to the party.

MAKES 12

Ingredients:
- 6 slices of bread
- margarine

For the fillings:

Cheese, Ham and Tomato
- 50 g (2 oz) cheddar cheese
- 2 slices of ham
- 1 large tomato, sliced

Egg Mayonnaise
- 1 egg
- 2 tablespoons mayonnaise
- salad (optional)

Chicken and Tomato
- 1/2 tomato
- 50 g (2 oz) cold chicken
- salad (optional)

1 First, spread the margarine on one side of each of the slices of bread. Next, start to layer up the filling insides.

2 Cheese, Ham and Tomato

Ask an adult to help you slice or grate the cheese. Place the cheese on one of the pieces of bread, followed by the ham. Add sliced tomato. Place another slice of bread on top and cut into four triangles.

3 Egg Mayonnaise

Place the egg in a saucepan half-filled with cold water and ask an adult to bring the water to a boil. Once the water is boiling, turn the heat down and let the egg simmer for about 7 minutes. When the egg has cooked, ask an adult to remove it from the hot water and let it cool. Carefully peel the shell off, then chop the egg into chunks. Put the egg chunks into a bowl and mix together with the mayonnaise. Spoon onto one of the pieces of bread. Add salad if you wish. Place another slice of bread on top and cut into four triangles.

4 Chicken and Tomato

Ask an adult to slice the tomato. Then, place the cold chicken on one of the pieces of bread, followed by a couple of slices of tomato. Add salad if you wish. Place another slice of bread on top and cut into four triangles.

DIPPY MOZZARELLA STICKS

Extra equipment:
• baking tray
• baking parchment

Ingredients:
• 450 g (1 lb) mozzarella
• 2 eggs
• 2 tablespoons plain flour
• 100 g (4 oz) breadcrumbs
• salt and pepper

For the salsa:
• 400 g (14 oz) tinned chopped tomatoes
• ½ red onion, chopped
• 1 tablespoon coriander
• 2 cloves garlic, peeled and crushed

1 Preheat the oven to 200°C / 400°F / gas mark 6.

2 Cut the mozzarella into strips about 2 cm (1 in.) wide.

3 Next, ask an adult to separate the egg yolk and whites. Discard the yolk, and place the whites in a bowl.

4 Place the flour and breadcrumbs into two separate bowls. Put a pinch of salt and pepper in the flour. Dip a mozzarella strip into the flour first, then into the egg whites and then the breadcrumbs.

5 Dip the stick into the egg again and then the breadcrumbs again. Try to make sure the cheese is completely covered.

6 Repeat with all the cheese sticks and then place on a baking tray lined with parchment. Bake for 10–15 minutes in the oven, turning occasionally, until golden.

7 To make the salsa: combine all of the salsa ingredients in a bowl and mix well.

8 Once the mozzarella sticks are cooked, serve with the dipping salsa!

TOP TIP!
These sticks also taste great with ketchup!

NACHOS & TOMATO SALSA

Extra equipment:
• baking tray

Ingredients:

For the salsa:
• 350 g (12 oz) fresh tomatoes
• 1/2 red onion, chopped
• 1 tablespoon coriander, chopped
• 2 cloves garlic, peeled and crushed

For the nachos:
• 1 large pack of tortilla crisps
• 50 g (2 oz) cheddar cheese, grated
• 1 jalapeno pepper, chopped (optional)

1 Preheat the grill to a medium heat.

To make the salsa:

2 Ask an adult to chop the tomatoes into small pieces, making sure that there are no seeds, and place into a bowl.

3 Place the remaining salsa ingredients into the bowl and mix together well before transferring into a small serving bowl.

To make the nachos:

4 Scatter the tortilla crisps onto a baking tray and sprinkle the cheese and chopped jalapenos over the top so the crisps are evenly covered.

5 Place the tortilla crisps on the baking tray under the preheated grill for 3–4 minutes, until the cheese has melted.

6 Dip your nachos into the salsa and enjoy a taste sensation!

TOP TIP! Why not add some guacamole and sour cream to your nachos!

CHEESY HAM POTATO SKINS

Extra equipment:
- baking tray
- pastry brush

Ingredients:
- 2 large potatoes
- 2 tablespoons olive oil
- 1 onion, chopped
- 1 tablespoon barbecue sauce (optional)
- 100 g (4 oz) cheddar cheese
- 6 slices of ham, cut into squares

1 Preheat the oven to 200°C / 400°F / gas mark 6. Scrub the large potatoes well and ask an adult to place them in the oven. Bake for 40–45 minutes until they feel slightly soft when squeezed. Leave to cool for a little while.

2 When cool, cut each potato in half. Scoop the inside out with a spoon (reserving for later), leaving a small layer of potato on the skin.

3 Brush inside and outside of the potato skins with a small amount of oil and place them back into the oven.

4 Bake for 15 minutes, turning halfway through, until crispy and golden brown.

5 While the potato skins are cooking, ask an adult to heat some oil in a frying pan and cook the onions until slightly soft.

6 Take the potato skins out of the oven and, if you wish, spread a small amount of barbecue sauce on each of the potato skins.

7 Mix the reserved potato, cooked onions, grated cheese and ham squares in a bowl.

8 Spoon the mixture evenly into the potato skins and place back in the oven for about 5 minutes, until the cheese has melted.

TOP TIP! Don't be afraid to experiment with different fillings!

PASTRY POCKETS

Extra equipment:
- rolling pin
- pastry brush
- baking tray

Ingredients:
- 375 g (13 oz) puff pastry
- 1 egg yolk (beaten with 1 tablespoon water)
- 450 g (1 lb) favourite cheese
- 3 large tomatoes, sliced
- 3 teaspoons of sesame seeds
- basil, to decorate (optional)

1 Preheat the oven to 200°C / 400°F / gas mark 6.

2 Roll out the pastry so it is 1/2 cm (1/4 in.) thick. Cut into 8 cm (3 in.) squares and brush the edges with beaten egg.

3 Cut the cheese into 20 slices. Put a slice onto each piece of pastry, followed by a slice of tomato.

4 Pinch together the corners of the pastry and flatten slightly.

5 Place the pastry onto an oiled baking tray and brush with more beaten egg. Sprinkle with sesame seeds.

6 Bake for 15 minutes in the oven, until the pastry has puffed up. Serve warm or at room temperature, decorated with basil.

TOP TIP!
Why not cut the pastry into different shapes, such as stars or hearts, or if you're having a themed party, cut the pastry parcels to reflect this theme!

CHUNKY WEDGES

Extra equipment:
• baking tray

Ingredients:
• 5 large potatoes
• 5 tablespoons olive oil
• chives, finely chopped

1 Preheat the oven to 200°C / 400°F / gas mark 6.

2 First, scrub the potatoes, but do not peel. Cut each potato in half and then each half into about three wedges.

3 Place the wedges into a heatproof bowl with a couple of inches of water and microwave for 5–10 minutes, until they are slightly soft.

4 Then, scatter the wedges onto a baking tray and drizzle with olive oil.

5 Ask an adult to place the baking tray into a preheated oven and cook for about 25–30 minutes until cooked through.

6 Ask an adult to stir the wedges around during cooking so they don't burn.

7 Sprinkle with finely chopped chives (optional). Serve hot!

TOP TIP! Chilli jam is the perfect accompaniment for chunky wedges.

FISHY FINGERS

Ingredients:

- 800 g (1 lb, 7 oz) haddock or pollack fillets, skinned and boned
- 100 g (4 oz) plain flour, seasoned with a pinch of salt and pepper
- 2 eggs, lightly beaten
- 200 g (7 oz) fresh breadcrumbs
- olive oil or rapeseed oil for shallow frying
- lemon wedges or tomato ketchup, to serve

1 Ask an adult to cut the fish fillets into 'fingers'.

2 Next, prepare three bowls, one containing the lightly seasoned flour, another containing the beaten eggs, and a third containing the fresh breadcrumbs.

3 One at a time, dust the fish fingers lightly with flour, shaking off any excess, then dip in the egg and finally, coat each finger thoroughly with breadcrumbs.

4 Ask an adult to place a frying pan over a medium heat with a few tablespoons of oil. Shallow fry the fish fingers for approximately 2–3 minutes each side until golden.

5 Serve with a squeeze of lemon or tomato ketchup.

TOP TIP!
Why not make some mushy peas to go with the fingers? Ask an adult to cook the peas, mash, add créme fraîche, then stir.

BARBECUE CHICKEN DRUMSTICKS

Extra equipment:
• baking tray

Ingredients:
• 1 teaspoon crushed red pepper
• 2 teaspoons cajun seasoning
• 1 teaspoon chilli powder
• 1/2 teaspoon cornflour
• 6 tablespoons brown sugar
• 100 ml (3 fl.oz) lemon juice
• 500 ml (17 fl.oz) orange juice
• 1 kg (2 lbs, 2 oz) chicken drumsticks
• 1 tablespoon oil

1 Preheat the oven to 180°C / 350°F / gas mark 4.

2 First, make the marinade by combining all of the dry ingredients. Mix together well, then add the lemon juice and orange juice and stir.

3 Place the chicken drumsticks in a deep bowl and cover with the barbecue marinade. Cover and refrigerate for at least 6 hours.

4 Remove the drumsticks from the marinade and place onto a baking tray. Place the marinade in a saucepan, and heat on a low setting until it has thickened.

5 Ask an adult to place the drumsticks in the oven for about 30–35 minutes, turning occasionally and basting with the sauce.

TOP TIP!
Be extra careful when handling raw chicken. Remember to thoroughly wash your hands immediately after you touch it.

WRAP SANDWICHES

MAKES 16

Ingredients:

- 8 flour tortilla wraps
- 4 tablespoons mayonnaise
- 4 slices of ham
- 50 g (2 oz) cheddar cheese, sliced
- 50 g (2 oz) green salad
- 2 large tomatoes, sliced
- 25 g (1 oz) cucumber, sliced
- 50 g (2 oz) cold chicken, chopped

1 Place the tortillas on a work surface and spread each one with mayonnaise.

2 Divide the filling among the tortillas and then roll up tightly.

3 Cut each rolled tortilla into 5 cm (2 in.) sections.

4 Serve on a brightly coloured plate and watch them all disappear!

TOP TIP! Chunky wedges (see page 21) are the perfect accompaniment for this recipe.

HEARTY HOT DOGS

Extra equipment:
• baking tray

Ingredients:
• 8 sausages
• bread rolls of your choice
• salad (optional)
• sauce, to serve (optional)

1 Preheat the oven to 180°C / 350°F / gas mark 4.

2 First, place the sausages onto the baking tray and cook for 20–25 minutes, asking an adult to turn halfway through the cooking time.

3 Meanwhile, ask an adult to open up the bread rolls with a knife.

4 Add any extra filling such as salad and then place a sausage into each roll.

5 Serve them on a plate, leaving sauces on the side (mustard shown).

TOP TIP! Serve hearty hot dogs with a fun salad face (see page 37).

MINI VEGETABLE SAMOSAS

TOP TIP!
This recipe is for mild samosas — if you want slightly spicier ones add more chilli!

MAKES 4

Extra equipment:
- pastry brush
- baking tray

Ingredients:
- 1/2 potato
- 1/2 carrot
- 1/2 onion, chopped
- 2 tablespoons oil
- 1/2 red chilli, chopped
- 2 teaspoons garam masala
- 1/2 teaspoon turmeric
- 30 ml (1 fl.oz) water
- 25 g (1 oz) peas (frozen)
- 1/2 teaspoon fresh coriander
- 1 pack filo pastry
- 25 g (1 oz) butter, melted

1 Preheat oven to 200°C / 400°F / gas mark 6.

2 First, ask an adult to peel and dice the potato and carrot into small chunks. Ask an adult to add to a saucepan filled with hot water and boil for 5–8 minutes.

3 Meanwhile, add the onion to a pan and ask an adult to fry in the oil for 4–5 minutes. Add the chilli and spices and cook for a further minute.

4 Drain the potatoes and carrots and add the potatoes, carrots and water to the onion mixture. Continue to fry gently for 5 minutes. Add the peas and coriander and then remove from the heat and allow to cool.

5 Lay 2–3 sheets of filo pastry on the work surface and ask an adult to cut into 10 cm (4 in.) wide strips. Brush with melted butter.

6 Place a tablespoon of filling in the bottom left-hand corner of each filo pastry strip and fold over to make a triangle. Repeat this process for the remaining samosas.

7 Place all of the samosas on a baking tray and brush with melted butter before baking for 10 minutes.

26

STUFFED PEPPERS

MAKES 4

Extra equipment:
• ovenproof dish

Ingredients:
• 100 g (4 oz) uncooked white long grain rice
• salt
• 2 tablespoons olive oil
• 1 onion, finely chopped
• 250 g (9 oz) beef mince
• 400 g (14 oz) tinned chopped tomatoes
• 4 large peppers
• 2 tablespoons fresh parsley, chopped

1 Preheat the oven to 180°C / 350°F / gas mark 4.

2 Place the rice in a saucepan of cold water, with a pinch of salt, and ask an adult to bring to the boil. Cook for 12 minutes, or until soft. Once cooked, drain the rice.

3 Heat the oil in a pan. Fry the onions and mince for about 5 minutes, until the onions are soft and the mince is brown. Stir in the tomatoes and cook for another 2 minutes.

4 Remove the saucepan from the heat and add the rice to the mixture. Mix well.

5 Ask an adult to cut the tops off the peppers and scoop out the seeds.

6 Spoon the mince mixture into the peppers.

7 Put the peppers into an ovenproof dish and then ask an adult to place in the oven for about 10–15 minutes. Sprinkle with parsley, and then serve!

TOP TIP!
Grated cheese makes a tasty topping for these peppers.

CHEESY SCONES

Extra equipment:
- baking tray
- rolling pin
- pastry cutter

Ingredients:
- 225 g (8 oz) self-raising flour
- pinch of salt
- 50 g (2 oz) butter
- 25 g (1 oz) mature cheddar cheese, grated
- 150 ml (5 fl.oz) milk

1 Preheat the oven to 200°C / 400°F / gas mark 6. Lightly grease a baking tray.

2 Mix together the flour and salt and rub in the butter.

3 Stir in the cheese, followed by the milk, to create a soft dough.

4 Knead the dough on a floured work surface. Then, roll out the dough until it is 2 cm (3/4 in.) thick.

5 Then, use a pastry cutter to cut out the scones and place them onto the baking tray. Brush the top of each scone with a little milk.

6 Ask an adult to place them into the preheated oven and bake for 12–15 minutes or until they have risen and are a nice golden colour.

7 Transfer the scones onto a wire rack and allow to cool.

TOP TIP!
Spread the scones with butter before serving.

28

PERFECT PASTA

Ingredients:

- olive oil
- 1 onion, chopped
- 1 clove of garlic, peeled and crushed
- 1 tablespoon tomato purée
- 400 g (14 oz) tinned chopped tomatoes
- fresh basil, chopped
- freshly ground black pepper
- 1/2 teaspoon sugar
- 300 g (10 oz) penne pasta
- Parmesan cheese (or your preferred type of cheese), to serve

1 Ask an adult to heat the olive oil in a large pan. Gently fry the onion and garlic on a low heat for a few minutes.

2 Next, add the tomato purée and cook for a further couple of minutes.

3 Add the chopped tomatoes, basil, black pepper and sugar, and then stir well. Cover the pan and leave to simmer for around 15 minutes.

4 Meanwhile, ask an adult to add the pasta to a saucepan filled with hot water. Boil for 10 minutes, or until it is just cooked.

5 Serve the tomato sauce over the pasta and top with grated Parmesan cheese.

TOP TIP! This pasta dish can be served hot or cold.

Extra equipment:
- cocktail sticks

Ingredients:
- 50 g (2 oz) grapes
- 50 g (2 oz) cheese of your choice

1 Ask an adult to chop the cheese into bite-sized square chunks.

2 Poke the cocktail sticks through the grapes, followed by the cheese chunks. Keep going until you have as many as you need!

TOP TIP!
Experiment and add different bite-sized treats, such as pineapple, olives and sausage!

CHEESE FONDUE

Extra equipment:
• fondue pot and sticks

Ingredients:
• ¹/₂ clove garlic
• 1 teaspoon lemon juice
• 225 g (8 oz) grated Gruyère cheese
• 225 g (8 oz) grated Emmenthal cheese
• 1 teaspoon cornflour
• black pepper, to taste
• cubes of bread, to serve

1 Rub the inside of the fondue pot with the cut clove of garlic. Put the lemon juice into the fondue pot and ask an adult to heat over a medium heat until bubbling.

2 Reduce the heat and carefully stir in the grated cheese. Keep stirring until all the cheese is melted and well combined. This takes a long time, but do not be tempted to turn up the heat, just keep stirring.

3 Add the cornflour to the cheese mixture. Cook for another two or three minutes, stirring constantly. Do not let the fondue boil. Season with black pepper.

4 Transfer to a table burner or pour into bowls to serve. Dip in the cubes of bread to serve.

TOP TIP!
If your fondue pot does not go on top of your cooker, you can make it in a saucepan instead and then transfer it to the fondue pot before bringing it to the table.

MINI QUICHES

Extra equipment:
- bun tin
- rolling pin
- round 10 cm (4 in.) pastry cutter

Ingredients:
- margarine or butter, for greasing
- 1 pack of ready made shortcrust pastry
- 2 eggs
- 150 ml (5 fl.oz) milk
- a pinch of herbs (optional)
- 50 g (2 oz) cheddar cheese, grated
- choice of fillings: tinned sweetcorn, chopped peppers, chopped cooked meat (ham, salami, chicken etc.), chopped mushrooms, frozen peas

1 Preheat the oven to 180°C / 350°F / gas mark 4.

2 Grease the bun tin with a little margarine. Next, roll the shortcrust pastry out until it is quite thin.

3 Cut out circles of pastry with the pastry cutter and then line the bun tin with the pastry circles. Re-roll any scraps to make more circles if needed.

4 Beat the eggs and milk together and then add the herbs (optional).

5 Place a little grated cheese in the bottom of each pastry case. Then add the fillings to each quiche.

6 Pour on the egg and milk mixture until it nearly reaches the top of the pastry.

7 Finally, ask an adult to place the bun tin in the preheated oven and bake for 15–25 minutes until lightly browned.

TOP TIP!
Prepare these quiches a day before to save time – they taste great cold.

VEGETABLE CRISPS

Extra equipment:
- swivel peeler or mandolin
- paper towels
- baking tray

Ingredients:
- 2 parsnips
- 2 beetroot
- 2 sweet potatoes
- 2 tablespoons of olive oil
- freshly ground salt and black pepper

1 Preheat the oven to 200°C / 400°F / gas mark 6.

2 Ask an adult to peel all of the vegetables. Using a swivel peeler or mandolin, carefully slice them diagonally into wafer-thin crisps. Spread out on paper towels to remove any excess moisture.

3 Tip all the vegetables into a bowl. Pour over the oil and sprinkle with the salt and black pepper. Toss with your hands to coat evenly.

4 Arrange in a single layer on a baking tray. Roast on the lowest shelf in the oven for 20 minutes, turning halfway through. They are ready when the parsnips and sweet potato are golden brown.

5 Spread out on paper towels until cool and crisp.

TOP TIP!
Veggie crisps taste great with hummus or cheese and chive dips.

MINI MEATBALLS

Extra equipment:
- 12 cocktail sticks

Ingredients:
- 400 g (14 oz) lean beef mince
- 1 onion, finely chopped
- 1 clove garlic, chopped
- 1 teaspoon dried oregano
- 1 teaspoon dried basil
- 1 egg, beaten
- 30 g (1 oz) breadcrumbs
- 1 tablespoon olive oil

1 Mix the mince, onion, garlic, herbs and egg in a bowl.

2 Gradually add the breadcrumbs until mixture is firm, yet moist. Roll the mixture into medium-sized balls with your hands.

3 Heat the olive oil in a pan over a medium heat and ask an adult to fry the meatballs until brown – keep them separated and be careful when you turn them to keep them from breaking.

4 Pour off any excess oil and leave to cool. Then, push a mini meatball onto each cocktail stick. Serve with a barbecue sauce or ketchup.

TOP TIP! You can make these meatballs with pork or turkey mince as well!

SAVOURY CRÊPES

Extra equipment:
- sieve
- ladle
- palette knife

Ingredients:
- 140 g (5 oz) plain flour
- 200 ml (7 fl.oz) whole milk
- 100 ml (3 fl.oz) water
- 2 eggs
- 25 g (1 oz) unsalted butter, melted, plus a little extra for greasing
- filling of your choice

1 Sift the flour into a medium-size bowl and make a well in the middle. Mix the milk and the water together. Break the eggs into the well and start whisking slowly. Add the milk and water in a steady stream, whisking constantly and gradually working in the flour from the sides of the bowl.

2 Whisk until the batter is smooth and all of the milk and water has been added. Set the batter aside to rest for 30 minutes, then whisk the melted butter into the batter.

3 Ask an adult to heat the pan. Very lightly grease the pan with melted butter. Using a ladle, pour roughly 2 tablespoons of batter into the pan and swirl it around so the bottom of the pan is evenly coated.

4 Cook the crêpe for about 45 seconds on one side until golden and then, using a palette knife, flip the crêpe over and cook the other side for about 30 seconds until it freckles.

5 Slide the crêpe out of the pan and top with your filling – in this case, ham, cooked spinach and grated cheese. Ask an adult to place under a preheated grill if you would like the cheese melted. Continue until all the batter is used up.

TOP TIP!
This recipe can also make sweet crêpes! Top with chocolate spread, bananas or ice cream for a sweet treat!

STAR SANDWICHES

Extra equipment:
• large star-shaped cookie cutter

Ingredients:
• 1 egg
• 2 tablespoons mayonnaise
• butter or margarine, to spread
• 4 slices bread, white or brown
• 2 slices of ham

1 First, make the egg mayonnaise filling. Place the egg in a saucepan half filled with cold water and ask an adult to bring the water to a boil.

2 Once the water is boiling, turn the heat down and let the egg simmer for about 7 minutes. When the egg has cooked, ask an adult to remove it from the hot water and let it cool.

3 Carefully peel the shell off, then mash the egg using a fork. Put the mashed egg into a bowl and mix together with the mayonnaise. Set aside for later.

4 Next, spread the butter or margarine onto the bread slices.

5 Next, layer the ham and egg mayonnaise onto one slice of bread then top with another slice.

6 Repeat with the next two slices of bread.

7 Use the cookie cutter to make star-shaped sandwiches.

TOP TIP! Don't forget to use other cookie cutters to make different shaped sandwiches!

36

SALAD FACES

Ingredients:
- iceberg lettuce
- lemon, sliced and chopped
- parsley sprigs
- black olives (or grapes)
- tomato, sliced

1 Wash your iceberg lettuce and lay one large leaf onto a plate.

2 Ask an adult to slice the lemon, reserving some for later, and place two slices onto the lettuce leaf.

3 Top with parsley sprigs and black olives for the eyes!

4 Next, ask an adult to slice the tomato and place it onto the leaf for a smiling mouth.

5 Then, chop some of the reserved lemon and place around the tomato to make teeth!

6 Why not use a variety of salad ingredients, such as sweetcorn, cucumber and different types of salad leaves to make different faces?

TOP TIP!
Use the salad face as the centre piece of a party food plate and serve other food at the side.

VEGGIE KEBABS

Extra equipment:
- wooden skewers
- pastry brush

Ingredients:
- 1 red onion
- 1 pepper, any colour
- 1 courgette
- 1 aubergine
- 6 cherry tomatoes
- 10 button mushrooms
- 2 tablespoons olive oil
- black pepper (optional)

1 Preheat the grill or barbecue to a medium heat.

2 First, prepare the vegetables. Ask an adult to chop the onion, pepper, courgette and aubergine into thick slices, leaving the tomatoes and button mushrooms whole.

3 Carefully push the vegetables onto the skewers, alternating the different types so the colour is varied.

4 Brush the vegetables with a little olive oil and sprinkle with black pepper (optional). Then, ask an adult to place the skewers onto a barbecue or under a hot grill until the vegetables have softened.

TOP TIP!
Try this with lots of different vegetables. Which combinations work best together?

DELI TOWERS

Extra equipment:
- cocktail sticks

Ingredients:
- 1 French stick or large baguette, cut into chunks
- 1 tub salmon paste
- 1/2 cucumber, sliced
- 100 g (4 oz) cooked ham, sliced
- olives (optional)

1 Starting with the French bread, build up the layers, adding the paste, cucumber slices, ham and olives.

2 Repeat until all of the ingredients have been used up.

3 Make sure the deli towers don't topple over by skewering each one with a cocktail stick.

TOP TIP!
Grapes and pineapple chunks make a nice alternative to the olives used in this dish.

MINI TOMATO BITES

Ingredients:
- 10 small tomatoes
- 1 tin of tuna
- 50 g (2 oz) white rice, cooked
- 25 g (1 oz) peas, cooked
- 25 g (1 oz) red pepper, finely chopped
- basil (optional)

1 First, wash the tomatoes, before placing them on a chopping board. Ask an adult to cut the tops of the tomatoes off. Scoop out the insides with a spoon.

2 Next, mix the tuna, rice, peas and red pepper in a bowl. Fill the tomatoes with the mixture.

3 Top with basil to finish and serve.

TOP TIP! Try this recipe with hollowed out red peppers – it makes a great main course for a summer barbecue party.

CHICKEN TOWERS

Extra equipment:
• cocktail sticks

Ingredients:
• 100 g (4 oz) pineapple, fresh or tinned, cut into chunks
• 100 g (4 oz) cooked chicken, cut into chunks
• basil leaves
• 2 tomatoes, sliced

1 First, take the pineapple chunks and place the chicken on top.

2 Add the basil on top of the chicken, followed by a slice of tomato. Add another chunk of chicken and finish with a smaller chunk of pineapple.

3 Repeat until all of the ingredients have been used up.

4 Use decorative cocktail sticks to prevent your chicken towers from toppling over.

TOP TIP! Try cooked gammon for a great variation on this tower recipe.

SPRING ROLLS

SERVES 4

TOP TIP!
Serve these scrummy spring rolls with sweet chilli dipping sauce!

Extra equipment:
- baking paper
- baking tray
- pastry brush

Ingredients:
- 50 g (2 oz) grated carrot
- 50 g (2 oz) tinned cannellini beans, rinsed
- 50 g (2 oz) fresh bean sprouts, chopped
- 1 spring onion
- 25 g (1 oz) mushrooms
- 1 tablespoon chilli dipping sauce
- 50 g (2 oz) cooked chicken, chopped
- vegetable oil
- 8 sheets square-shaped filo pastry

1 Preheat the oven to 200°C / 400°F / gas mark 6.

2 Put the grated carrot, beans and bean sprouts into a bowl and mix together well. Ask an adult to chop the spring onion and mushrooms into small pieces. Add these to the carrot, beans and bean sprouts and mix. Stir in 1 tablespoon of chilli dipping sauce and add the chicken.

3 Put some baking paper on a baking tray and brush with oil. Now take out eight sheets of filo pastry. Place one sheet on a clean surface and dab it all over with oil. Place another piece on top. Dab this piece with oil too.

4 Turn the pastry with your hands so that a corner is pointing towards you (like a diamond). Spoon some of the filling onto the corner nearest you. Fold this corner towards the centre and tuck it under the filling. Fold the two outside corners in towards the middle so it looks like an envelope.

5 Dab with oil and then roll up the pastry to look like a sausage. Dab with more oil and put on the baking tray. Repeat until you have made four.

6 Ask an adult to place the baking tray in the preheated oven for 15–20 minutes until crisp and golden.

MINI FRITTATA

Extra equipment:
• 12-hole muffin tray

Ingredients:
• olive oil
• 50 g (2 oz) spring onions, sliced
• 100 g (4 oz) red pepper, chopped
• 1 teaspoon dried oregano
• 200 g (7 oz) potatoes, cooked and chopped
• 8 free-range eggs
• 100 g (4 oz) cheddar cheese, grated

1 Preheat the oven to 200°C / 400°F / gas mark 6. Grease a non-stick 12-hole muffin tray with oil.

2 Ask an adult to heat some oil in a pan, and then add the onions, red pepper and oregano. Cook for a few minutes until tender and golden.

3 Then stir in the cooked potato and leave to cool.

4 Meanwhile, break the eggs into a jug, whisk and stir in the cheese.

5 Divide the vegetable mixture between the muffin holes and pour the egg and cheese mixture on top.

6 Bake for 15 mins until puffed, golden and set. Leave to cool slightly then pop out of the tray.

7 Cut the frittatas into bite-sized pieces or leave them whole.

TOP TIP!
Add chopped ham to this recipe in step 2 for party carnivores!

MINI CHICKEN BURGERS

Extra equipment:
- food processor

Ingredients:
- 450 g (1 lb) chicken mince
- 2–3 cloves garlic, peeled and crushed
- 25 g (1 oz) Italian flat leaf parsley
- 1/2 tsp dried oregano
- 1/2 tsp dried basil
- 1/2 lemon, juice only
- salt and pepper
- 6–8 mini burger buns
- salad (optional)

1. In a large bowl, thoroughly combine the chicken mince, garlic, parsley, oregano, basil and lemon juice. Season with salt and pepper. Ask an adult to place the ingredients in a food processor and mix.

2. Once mixed, mould the chicken mixture into about 6–8 patties, about 5 cm (2 in.) in diameter.

3. Ask an adult to heat the oil in a frying pan over a medium heat. Cook the patties for 8–10 minutes until they are browned on each side and cooked through.

4. Meanwhile, layer the mini buns with salad, if using. Once the burgers are cooked, place on top of the bottom bun and sandwich with the other half.

TOP TIP! This recipe also works well with turkey mince.

POTATO SALAD

Ingredients:

- 675 g (1 lb 8 oz) new potatoes, scrubbed
- 8 tablespoons salad cream
- 1/2 red onion, chopped (optional)
- 50 g (2 oz) spring onions, sliced (optional)
- 1 hard-boiled egg, chopped

1 Put the new potatoes in a saucepan of water, ask an adult to bring to the boil and leave to simmer for 20–25 minutes.

2 When cooked, drain the potatoes, chop into smaller pieces and put them in a large brightly-coloured serving bowl. Leave the potatoes to cool and then add the salad cream, stirring until the potatoes are completely coated.

3 Next, add both types of onion and chopped egg, again stirring until covered.

TOP TIP!
Replace the salad cream with mayonnaise for a less sweet variation of this dish.

PIGS IN BLANKETS

Extra equipment:
- baking tray

Ingredients:
- 16 rashers smoked streaky bacon
- 36 small sausages
- rosemary sprigs (optional)

1 Preheat the oven to 180°C / 350°F / gas mark 4.

2 Using the back of a knife, ask an adult to stretch each bacon rasher out – this will stop them from shrinking as they cook.

3 Cut each rasher in half horizontally and roll a piece around a sausage. Place them on a non-stick baking tray.

4 Bake for 35–40 minutes, asking an adult to turn them once, until brown and piping hot.

5 Once cooked, serve, adding sprigs of rosemary if desired.

TOP TIP!
A plum dipping sauce is a great accompaniment for this popular party dish.

CRUNCHY COLESLAW

Extra equipment:
• food processor or vegetable shredder

Ingredients:
• 180 g (6 oz) white cabbage
• 1 medium carrot, peeled
• 2 tablespoons mayonnaise

1 First, gather together the vegetables that you are going to shred: in this case, the white cabbage and the carrot.

2 Set the food processor to the shred setting and place the vegetables inside before blitzing.

3 If you haven't got a food processor, shred your vegetables by hand using a vegetable shredder or ask an adult to use a sharp knife.

4 Toss the vegetables together in a large bowl.

5 Store the coleslaw in the fridge until you are ready to serve and then dress with the mayonnaise.

6 Mix well just before serving.

TOP TIP! Use red cabbage for a more colourful variation of this dish.

BEJEWELLED COUSCOUS

SERVES 4-6

Ingredients:
- 225 g (8 oz) couscous
- 2 large tomatoes
- 1 large yellow pepper

1 Cover the couscous with twice its volume of hot water and leave to soak for 10 minutes.

2 Meanwhile, start to prepare the vegetables. Wash them first and then ask an adult to chop them up into small pieces.

3 When the couscous has absorbed all of the water, mix in the vegetables.

4 Leave to stand for 30 minutes to let the flavours develop, then serve.

TOP TIP!
Don't be afraid to add more brightly coloured ingredients such as cucumber, red and green peppers and apricots!

PIZZA BAGUETTES

Extra equipment:
• baking tray

Ingredients:
• 1 tablespoon vegetable oil
• 2 rashers bacon
• 400 g (14 oz) tinned chopped tomatoes or the same amount of fresh tomatoes, skinned and chopped
• 1 garlic clove, peeled and crushed
• 2 fresh basil leaves
• 2 baguettes or ciabatta
• 1 tablespoon olive oil (optional)
• 50 g (2 oz) cheddar cheese, grated

1 Preheat the oven to 180°C / 350°F / gas mark 4.

2 Heat the oil in a frying pan and add the bacon. Fry for 5 minutes, turning halfway. Leave to cool, then ask an adult to chop the bacon into pieces.

3 Next, mix the tomatoes, garlic and basil together in a bowl. Then, gently heat in a saucepan.

4 Split the baguettes in half and spread the tomato mixture on top.

5 Drizzle with a little olive oil, if desired, then sprinkle with grated cheese and the bacon bits.

6 Place on a baking tray and put the pizzas in the oven for about 10 minutes or until the cheese has melted and the bread is hot.

TOP TIP!
Chopped pineapple makes a great topping addition to this recipe.

49

MINI PASTIES

Extra equipment:
- large round cookie cutters
- 2 baking trays
- baking parchment

Ingredients:
- 1 small swede, peeled
- 1 small carrot, peeled
- 1 small onion, peeled
- 1 medium potato, peeled
- 400 g (14 oz) beef mince
- 50 g (2 oz) frozen peas
- 1 teaspoon salt
- freshly cracked pepper
- 6–7 sheets frozen puff pastry, thawed
- 1 egg, lightly beaten
- sesame seeds, to decorate (optional)

1 Preheat the oven to 200°C / 400°F / gas mark 6.

2 Ask an adult to chop the swede, carrot, onion and potato into small cubes. Put the cubes into a bowl.

3 Add the beef mince, peas, salt and pepper. Mix well to combine.

4 Cut the pastry into rounds using the cookie cutter.

5 Add one heaped tablespoon of the mince mixture into the centre of the pastry rounds. Using the lightly beaten egg, brush the egg wash around the edges of the filled pastry rounds.

6 Then pull up the edges of the pastry over the mixture and pinch at the top and down the sides to seal.

7 Place the pasties on baking trays, lined with baking parchment, and brush the tops with the beaten egg, followed by sesame seeds, if using.

8 Ask an adult to place the pasties in the preheated oven and cook for 35 minutes or until golden brown. Cool on a wire rack and serve.

TOP TIP!
These pasties are great eaten hot or cold!

MINI JACKET POTATOES

Extra equipment:
• baking tray

Ingredients:
• 12 potatoes
• olive oil
• 200 g (7 oz) cheddar cheese
• topping ingredients of your choice

1 Preheat the oven to 180°C / 350°F / gas mark 4.

2 Lightly grease a large baking tray and ask an adult to place the potatoes on the tray. Rub the potatoes with oil and then bake for 45–50 minutes, or until tender when a skewer is inserted into the centre.

3 Once the potatoes are cooked, preheat the grill.

4 Ask an adult to cut each potato in half. Using a tea towel, hold one potato. Squeeze the base gently to open the top. Repeat with the remaining potatoes.

5 Top with cheddar cheese and any other ingredients you fancy and grill for 2 minutes until the cheese has melted.

TOP TIP! Ham, cheese, tomato and sweetcorn make great potato toppings.

SAUSAGE BITES

Extra equipment:
- 24 cocktail sticks

Ingredients:
- 1 French stick
- 100 g (4 oz) spicy sausage, i.e. chorizo
- 75 g (3 oz) cheddar cheese
- 1 green pepper
- butter or margarine to spread

1 First, ask an adult to slice the French stick into small bite-sized slices.

2 Now slice the spicy sausage and cheese into small pieces.

3 Wash the green pepper and then chop into small chunks also.

4 Spread a little butter or margarine onto each bread slice.

5 Then, start to build up the bites. Place a sausage slice on top of the bread, followed by a cube of cheese and finally a piece of pepper. Use a cocktail stick to hold each bite in place.

6 Repeat until the remaining ingredients have been used up.

TOP TIP!
If you're not a fan of spicy food, use any other kind of meat, or even veggie sausage instead!

TASTY TARTLETS

Ingredients:
- 1/2 red onion, chopped
- 2 tomatoes, chopped
- 1 pepper, yellow or red, chopped
- 12 pre-bought cooked pastry cases
- basil leaves, to decorate

1 Ask an adult to help you wash and prepare the vegetables. Carefully cut them up into small chunks.

2 Fill the pastry cases, adding a selection of vegetables so each case gets a mixture.

3 Top with basil leaves to finish.

TOP TIP!
Why not add some cheese to the cases and ask an adult to place them under a grill for 2 minutes?

MINI FISHCAKES

Ingredients:
- 350 g (12 oz) tinned wild salmon
- 450 g (1 lb) mashed potato
- 2 tablespoons fresh parsley, finely chopped
- juice of 1/2 lemon
- 1 small onion, grated
- salt and freshly ground black pepper
- 1 egg, beaten

To coat:
- 2 tablespoons plain flour
- 2 eggs, beaten
- 75 g (3 oz) breadcrumbs

To cook:
- 2 tablespoons oil

1 Drain the tinned salmon and put into a bowl. Mash with a fork, removing any large bones.

2 Add the mashed potato, followed by the parsley, lemon juice, onion, salt, pepper and egg.

3 Dust your hands with flour and mould the mixture into 15–18 mini cakes.

4 Coat each cake in flour, then dip into beaten egg and finally into the breadcrumbs. Set aside in the fridge for at least one hour so the fishcakes can set.

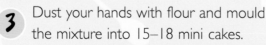

5 Ask an adult to heat 2 tablespoons of oil in a deep frying pan and cook the fishcakes over a medium heat, a few at a time, for 2–3 minutes on each side until golden brown and crisp.

TOP TIP!
This recipe works just as well with tinned tuna.

BRUSCHETTA BITES

MAKES 12

Extra equipment:
• baking tray

Ingredients:
• half a baguette
• 4 tablespoons olive oil
• 8 large tomatoes
• basil leaves to garnish (optional)
• black pepper (optional)

1 Preheat the oven to 150°C / 325°F / gas mark 3.

2 Slice the baguette into about 12 (1.5 cm / 1/2 in.) thick slices and then discard the end pieces. Place the slices on a large baking tray.

3 Drizzle half of the olive oil over the top side of the bread, turn over the slices and drizzle with the remaining oil.

4 Bake the bread for 10 minutes until it is golden and crisp. Ask an adult to remove it from the oven and cool slightly.

5 Meanwhile, ask an adult to chop up the tomatoes and place into a bowl.

6 Once cool, arrange the bruschetta on a serving platter and then top each with the chopped tomatoes.

7 Finally decorate with basil leaves and a sprinkling of black pepper, if desired.

TOP TIP!
Turn to page 18 for instructions on how to make your own salsa – a great alternative to chopped tomatoes!

VEGETABLE POTS

Extra equipment:
• colourful pots

Ingredients:
• baby carrots
• 1 cucumber
• 1 red pepper
• 1 celery stick

1 First, wash and prepare the vegetables.

2 Ask an adult to peel the baby carrots.

3 Then chop the cucumber, pepper and celery into slices.

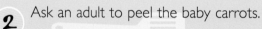

4 Once the vegetables are ready, place them upright in the colourful pots – ready for dipping.

5 Leave a selection of dips out!

TOP TIP!
Why not make your own brightly coloured pots using card and leftover wrapping paper?

SANDWICH FACES

Ingredients:
- 12 slices of bread, white or brown
- margarine, to spread
- a combination of filling ingredients

1 First, spread each slice of bread with margarine.

2 Then, start to add the filling combinations, layering each ingredient so that it looks like a face. We have used cooked ham, ready sliced cheese, olives for the eyes and nose and salad and tomatoes for the hair and mouth.

TOP TIP!
Have fun making the funniest faces you can think of!

CHICKEN GOUJONS

Extra equipment:

- deep fat fryer (see top tip if you don't have one)
- slotted spoon
- paper towels

Ingredients:

- 50 g (2 oz) plain flour
- 3 eggs, beaten
- 125 g (4 1/2 oz) fresh fine breadcrumbs
- 4 boneless and skinless chicken breasts, cut into thin strips

1 Ask an adult to heat a deep fat fryer to 190°C / 375°F.

2 Place the flour, egg and breadcrumbs in three separate bowls.

3 Dip the chicken strips in the flour, then dip into the beaten egg.

4 Then, dip the chicken into the breadcrumbs, making sure the chicken is coated thoroughly.

5 Ask an adult to place the goujons into the deep fat fryer in batches and cook for about 3–4 minutes, until crisp and golden brown and the chicken is completely cooked through. Carefully remove with a slotted spoon and drain onto paper towels.

6 Repeat until all the goujons are cooked and then serve.

TOP TIP!
If you don't have a deep fat fryer, ask an adult to place the goujons in a preheated oven to cook for 10–12 minutes, or until golden brown.

HAM & CHEESE PINWHEELS

Extra equipment:
• cling film

Ingredients:
• 260 g (9 oz) cream cheese
• 3 large soft flour tortillas about 24 cm (9 in.) diameter
• 12 thin slices of ham

1 Spread the cream cheese onto each tortilla, followed by three slices of ham.

2 Then roll the tortilla up into a really tight sausage shape. Wrap tightly in cling film and put into the fridge to firm up.

3 Cut the tortilla into small slices about 1 cm (1/2 in.) wide and serve on a platter.

TOP TIP!
The longer you leave the pinwheels in the fridge to chill, the easier they will be to cut.

BRILLIANT BREADSTICKS

MAKES 60

Extra equipment:
- sieve
- rolling pin
- 2–3 baking trays
- clean tea towel

Ingredients:
- 500 g (1 lb) strong plain flour
- 1 teaspoon salt
- 7 g sachet dried active yeast
- 300 ml (10 fl.oz) water (lukewarm)
- semolina, to sprinkle on the baking trays
- 1 egg, beaten
- 2 tablespoons water
- 1–2 tablespoons sesame seeds

1 Preheat the oven to 200°C / 400°F / gas mark 6.

2 Sift the flour into a bowl and stir in the salt and yeast. Pour 300 ml (10 fl.oz) of lukewarm water into the flour and mix well until it forms a dough.

3 Lightly flour a work surface and knead the dough for about 5–10 minutes, until it is smooth and elastic.

4 Divide the dough in half and roll each piece to about 20 x 30 cm (8 x 12 in.) and then cut widthways into strips about 1 cm (1/2 in.) thick.

5 Sprinkle the baking trays with the semolina, place the strips on top and then cover with a clean tea towel. Leave in a warm place until doubled in size.

6 Mix the egg and 2 tablespoons of water together, then brush the glaze over the strips of dough. Sprinkle with sesame seeds.

7 Bake for 12–15 minutes or until the breadsticks are pale golden in colour.

8 Ask an adult to remove the baking trays from the oven and transfer the sticks onto wire racks to cool.

CHICKEN FAJITA WRAPS

MAKES 8

Extra equipment:
- cling film

Ingredients:

For the salsa:
- 350 g (12 oz) fresh tomatoes
- 1/2 red onion, chopped
- 1 tablespoon coriander, chopped
- 2 cloves garlic, peeled and crushed

For the filling:
- 2 tablespoons olive oil
- 4 chicken breasts, cut into thin strips
- 2 tablespoons fajita seasoning
- 1 red onion, chopped
- 2 garlic cloves, crushed
- 1 red pepper, deseeded and sliced
- 1 orange or yellow pepper, deseeded and sliced
- 8 soft flour tortillas

To make the salsa:

1 Ask an adult to chop the tomatoes into small pieces, making sure there are no seeds, and tip into a bowl.

2 Place the remaning salsa ingredients into the bowl and mix together well before transferring to a small serving bowl.

To make the filling:

1 Ask an adult to heat the oil in a large frying pan, and add the chicken strips. Brown the chicken and then sprinkle with fajita seasoning.

2 Turn the heat down and add the onion and garlic. Cook gently for 5 minutes, and then add the peppers.

3 Put the flour tortillas onto a plate and cover with cling film.

4 Next, put the tortillas into the microwave and heat for 30 seconds.

5 Remove the chicken and vegetables from the heat, pile into the warm tortillas, add the salsa and roll, tucking in the ends.

TOP TIP!
Serve with grated cheese and sour cream.

CHICKPEA BURGERS

Extra equipment:
• food processor

Ingredients:
• 400 g (14 oz) tin chickpeas, rinsed and drained
• 1 small red onion, roughly chopped
• garlic clove, chopped
• handful of parsley
• 1 teaspoon ground cumin
• 1 teaspoon ground coriander
• ½ teaspoon harissa paste or chilli powder (optional)
• 2 tablespoons plain flour
• salt
• 2 tablespoons sunflower oil

1 First, pat the chickpeas dry with kitchen paper. Tip into a food processor along with the onion, garlic, parsley, spices, flour and a little salt. Blend until fairly smooth.

2 Then, shape the mixture into four patties with your hands.

3 Ask an adult to heat the oil in a frying pan, add the burgers, then quickly fry for 3 minutes on each side until lightly golden.

TOP TIP!
Why not serve with toasted pittas, yogurt or tomato salsa and a green salad?

SOFT PRETZELS

Extra equipment:
- baking tray
- pastry brush

Ingredients:
- 375 ml (12 1/2 fl.oz) warm water
- 1 teaspoon sugar
- 2 1/4 teaspoons dried active yeast
- 565 g (1 lb 4 oz) white bread flour
- 1 egg, whisked
- 1 teaspoon salt

1 Preheat the oven to 200°C / 400°F / gas mark 6.

2 First, combine the warm water and sugar. Then, add the yeast and let the mixture stand until it starts to bubble up.

3 Combine the yeast mixture, flour and salt to form a dough that is soft but not too sticky.

4 Knead for 10 minutes and then divide the dough into 10 equal pieces. Roll with your hands and shape into pretzel plait shapes (see picture) and place on a greased baking tray.

5 Carefully brush the pretzels with egg and then sprinkle with salt.

6 Bake in a preheated oven for 20–25 minutes, or until golden brown.

TOP TIP!
Dip these pretzels in melted chocolate for a sweet treat!

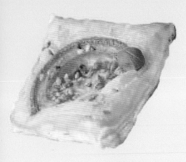

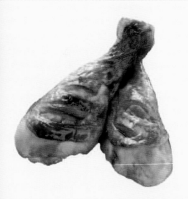

INDEX OF RECIPES

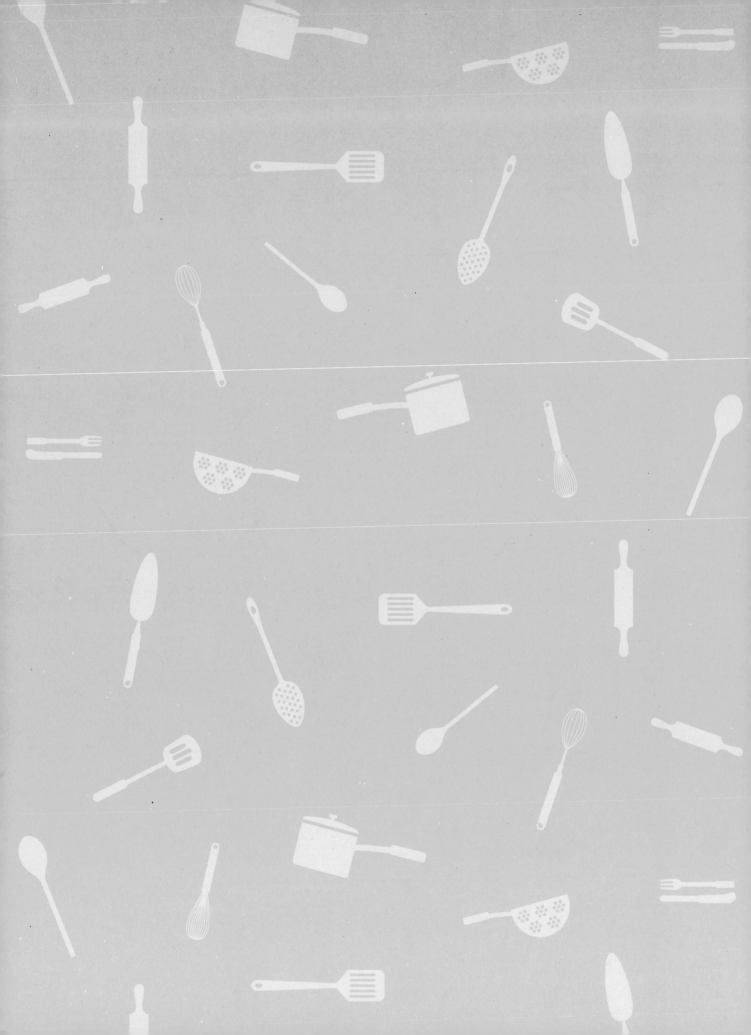